LITTLE BOOK OF

# OUTDOOR
# SURVIVAL

LITTLE BOOK OF
# OUTDOOR
# SURVIVAL

First published in the UK in 2012

© Demand Media Limited 2012

www.demand-media.co.uk

Printed and bound in China

ISBN 978-1-909217-09-6

# Contents

# Introduction

It's unlikely that any of us will actually need survival training. We live a relatively stress-free life in our comfortable homes and rarely venture into the back of beyond. But what would we do, and how would we cope, if the unthinkable happened and our aeroplane crashed in remote wilderness while we were going on holiday, or our cruise ship ran aground, or we became hopelessly lost while out walking in the Highlands, or we were caught in an avalanche while skiing off piste?

Thankfully, these situations don't arise very often, but they do happen. Our armed forces are trained to cope in such circumstances, but shouldn't we all have some basic survival training? We never know when we might need it.

According to the US Army's Field Manual, the first thing you should do is to assess the situation. For soldiers and other members of the military, this usually means finding somewhere safe from the enemy as you are likely to be in a combat environment. For the casual walker who's become lost, or the survivor of a car crash, this means using your senses to get a feel for what's happening, assessing your own physical condition and working out where you are.

The first problem is making sure you're out of immediate danger; the second is making sure you're physically able; and the third is working out how to deal with your situation and make

**Above:** Ice fishing in Finland.

it to safety. Every environment, be it jungle, desert, snowfield or wilderness, has a rhythm of sights and sounds and smells. Stay observant and tune into your surroundings to make sure you're safe.

Then you need to check to make sure you're not seriously injured. The shock of finding yourself in an accident or plunged unexpectedly into a survival situation can often cause the body to ignore the pain from life-threatening wounds. If you are injured, you will need to treat the wounds before you will be able to think about making your escape, so prioritising is another key survival technique.

If you are with other people, you'll need to make sure they are all okay too. To do this, think of Dr ABC. D is for danger: make sure the victim is safe from fire, falling rocks, drowning etc. R is for response: shout the person's name and check for a pain response by pinching their upper ear.

A is for airway: tilt the head back a little to make sure the airway isn't obstructed by the tongue or something they might have ingested. B is for breathing: if the patient is not breathing you'll need to perform CPR. C is for circulation, which can be checked via the carotid pulse on the side of the neck.

Provided you (and your team) are mobile, the three most important, but by no means the only, factors for staying alive are finding shelter, water and food, in that order. To accomplish this, you will almost always need to master the art of making fire: warmth is good for keeping you alive and raises morale. It will also help you cook food, sterilise water for drinking, signal for help, dry your clothes and keep insects and predators away. It is therefore a key ingredient of survival training.

It is never a good idea to rush. In your haste, you may overlook something important or forget something vital. In most cases of people getting lost while driving in the Australian outback, it is best to stay with the vehicle and await rescue, but too many people take their most precious belongings and head off on foot without any real thought as to where they're going. This is almost always a poor decision. The vehicle offers shelter and is more visible to search parties from the air and the ground. Belongings may have sentimental value, but they probably won't help you stay alive. And the car may well have useful tools and a water bottle, which, even if it isn't drinkable, may help to keep you cool.

To the casual traveller this next point may sound unimportant, but it always pays to know where you are. If you're out walking or driving, you will probably have started from a well-known base and will know roughly where you are in relation to local landmarks or points of interest, but what if you were skiing in the back country and were caught in a blizzard, or your plane came down in a swamp? Would you then be able to find your way back to civilisation? Making intelligent decisions in crises will certainly help you live longer. But your greatest enemies may still be out there: fear and panic.

Survivors need to eliminate both as quickly as possible. They can be stimulated by reaction to your feelings and imagination rather than by the cold reality of the survival situation you're facing. Fear and panic drain you mentally and trigger negative emotions. Most people who survive life-threatening situations do so because they have a clear head, a positive outlook and have the ability to remain calm under pressure. These attributes lead to good decision-making, which will help you make the correct choices at key points.

In our modern world, we have everything at our fingertips. If we break something, we, as creatures of comfort and habit, pop out and buy a new one. We are no longer the hunter-gatherers who improvised tools and strategies, and

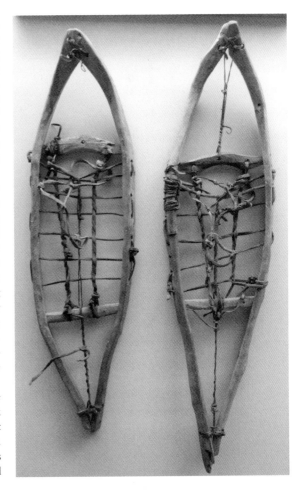

we dislike inconvenience and discomfort. Most survival situations are stressful and uncomfortable, and we don't have the tools we need for the job. In these instances, we need to learn to improvise and adapt, and to overcome obstacles that we would never face in our everyday lives.

Learning basic skills now will always pay off should the worst happen. If you know where you're heading, you can tailor your survival training to that environment. That training will give you confidence in your own ability and reduce the fear of the unknown. It will also prepare you to live by your wits, through ingenuity and determination, and give you the ability to think your way out of your predicament.

If you're caught unprepared by a train crash, there's probably not much you can do but improvise, but if you've headed into hiking territory deliberately you should always carry a few basic pieces of kit: a knife and other multi-function tools (which should always be kept clean); a water bottle for storing fluids; a compass (some people carry mobile phones with GPS but an old-fashioned compass can be just as useful, especially when your battery runs out); a flint and striker to make fire; a condom

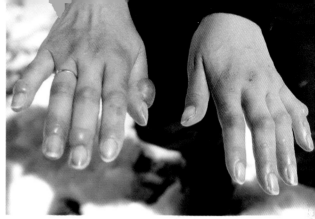

(aside from being able to carry up to two pints – 1.25 litres – of fluid, they can be used to protect injuries); a needle and thread to mend material, make snares and hooks; a small candle with matches; tampons can be used as tinder and to dress wounds; water sterilisation tablets; razor blades for skinning and gutting; a whistle; a mirror for signalling; wire and para cord for snares and lashing for shelters; a magnifying glass; a head torch; butterfly sutures for dressing wounds; duct tape; a tin mug and a plastic spoon; sunglasses and sun cream; and a hat.

Your rucksack will also need to be suitable. Those with several external pouches are usually best. Make sure everything you pack is waterproof and stored in high-quality re-sealable plastic bags. Choose one that's just big enough. If you buy something too large, you'll end up filling it with non-essential items. You should always carry a quality tent, hammock and poncho, and a few bungee straps.

You'll never get anywhere without a good pair of boots, but make sure they're well worn in by the time you need them. If you're heading for colder climes, make sure the boots are too big as you might need to wear several pairs of socks. You should usually choose boots with high uppers (to keep out mud and water), plenty of ankle support and, if climbing over rocky ground, a good Vibram sole. Choose woollen socks over nylon every time. And your clothing should be made from tough natural fibres. A synthetic sleeping bag may be bulkier and not as comfortable as those filled with natural goose down but it will be easier to dry and maintain.

**Above:**
Frostbitten hands.

**Above Left:**
The mighty west face of Siula Grande in Peru.

**Far Left:**
The angelica plant has edible roots.

**Above:** There are many different dangers to be aware of in nature.

# Surviving the Mountains

Millions of tourists ski, climb and trek in the mountain regions all over the world, but some are ill-equipped to deal with the weather and terrain, and hundreds are caught out each year. Some survive but others are not so fortunate. Mountains can be beautiful and spectacular but they can also be deadly.

The greatest threat to skiers is an avalanche: 40 people are killed each year in North America, with double that number in the European Alps, and another 40 die elsewhere, usually in avalanches they've triggered themselves. Many of these deaths could be avoided if the skiers and hikers had the know-how to read the snow conditions. A simple ski-pole test to make sure the snow layer is solid and consistent is usually enough. If the pole breaks through several layers, then that is a warning sign that the slope might be prone to avalanche.

You can also dig an avalanche pit to assess the snow conditions deeper underfoot. Dig a horizontal line in the soft top snow until you reach the base underneath. Then carve out vertical seams on either side before completing a block that should be about two feet (60 centimetres) square. If the block takes your weight when you hang from the top lip, there's a strong bond between the snow on the surface and the hard packed snow underneath. If it slides off easily, however, the bond may be weak

**Above:**
Crevasses on the
Price Glacier.

and the slope about to avalanche.

Sadly, many skiers and snowboarders don't take a few minutes to test the snow and end up triggering the avalanches that claim their lives. Also, if it is clear that the area has avalanched before, you should avoid crossing any slope steeper than 30 degrees.

If you are caught in an avalanche, conventional wisdom says that you should try to 'swim' on its surface and keep your head above the snow at all times. When avalanches stop, the snow sets like concrete, so it is vital to be near the surface. If you're buried and your arms are free, try to carve out a breathing area in front of your face. If you've become disoriented, spit to find out which way is up and then dig in that direction. If you can't move, you usually only have a maximum of 25 minutes before you will suffocate.

You can help your chances of survival by carrying some basic equipment, however. An avalanche transceiver sends out a signal to your companions and will guide them to you. An avalanche probe (an extendable rod) will help you pierce the snow and a shovel will help you dig out a friend who is buried. For obvious reasons, it is extremely unwise to ski in avalanche-prone areas at times of high risk, and it is even more foolish to do so alone. If it is unavoidable, always tell someone where you are going and when you intend to return.

If you have survived an avalanche, or if you have simply got lost on the mountain, you will doubtless face the dangers of hypothermia and frostbite. The extremities, such as the fingers and toes, and the exposed areas like the face will be the first to turn a waxy reddish colour. If untreated, minor frostbite can turn serious within 15 minutes. The skin then turns black and may, in the worst case scenario, need to be amputated. It is therefore vital to carry adequate protection for the hands and feet, as well as hoods and scarves for the face.

Hypothermia can kill if your core body temperature falls too low. With a two-degree loss, your words can become slurred, your coordination begins to suffer and you'll make a number of poor decisions. Severe shivering will follow as your body desperately tries to create heat through friction within your muscles. If your core temperature continues to fall below 32°C (92°F), skin colour fades and the extremities, particularly the lips, ears, fingers and toes, may turn blue. As the core temperature drops further, shivering stops as blood is diverted to keep the main organs alive. In a state of extreme confusion, some victims believe they are overheating and remove their clothes, hastening the inevitable.

In the mountains, wind can be as much of an enemy as low temperatures. High winds make it seem a lot colder so it's vital to take shelter. If wind speeds suddenly increase or they change direction, take extra care because you could be approaching cliffs. In the poor visibility of a whiteout, this can be fatal. The wind can help you maintain your direction, however. Ice particles on exposed rock usually face into the prevailing wind. Never underestimate the power of the wind and the weather it can bring. Exposure can kill in a few hours. The rocks may provide another clue about where you're heading. In

**Far Left:** Building a snow cave in the Antarctic.

the northern hemisphere moss clings to the north facing sides of rocks because they receive less sunlight and retain their moisture.

If the weather closes in or night approaches, it's likely that the ambient temperature will fall further so, if possible, it is vital to lose as much altitude as you can before finding shelter (temperatures rise approximately two degrees Celsius for every 300 metres descended, or four degrees Fahrenheit for every 1,000 feet). If the slopes are covered with snow, and you need to descend quickly, mountaineers use a technique called a glissade, which involves lying on your back and sliding down using your ice axe to slow the descent. Skiers can also use the technique, using their ski poles instead of an ice axe. It is risky in poor visibility because there may be unseen dangers like cliffs, but, in an emergency, it may be your only choice. If the terrain is uneven or rocky, a slow descent on foot will be your only option.

If you can't make it down and are not acclimatised to the environment, you need to monitor your physical and mental condition for signs of altitude sickness. If you start experiencing headaches and breathlessness, you should take time to rest and recover, but the most important thing is to climb down to a lower altitude where there is more oxygen. If this is not possible, exhaustion can soon overcome you and, if you haven't the energy to make a snow cave, you may die from exposure.

Snow caves are best made on lee slopes out of the wind because the snow will be thicker and easier to dig out. This is another time when your shovel will come in handy. Scoop the snow out of the bank and try to create a small platform above the level of the entrance. When the hollow is about three times the size of your body, crawl onto the platform. Your body heat will warm the raised area, while cooler air will sink into the depression away from you. Lying on a jacket or any spare clothing will also help preserve body heat as you lose 75% of it to the ground. Save any big blocks created during the excavation to shore up the entrance when you're inside, but remember to leave a small hole for ventilation to prevent suffocation.

A snow cave saved the lives of New Zealanders Mark Inglis and climbing partner Philip Doole when they got caught in an intense blizzard near the summit of Aoraki (Mount Cook) for

13 days in 1982. Their rescue made headlines around the world but they both suffered severe frostbite and Inglis had to have both legs amputated below the knee. Twenty years later he climbed the mountain with prosthetic limbs, and he would later summit Mount Everest.

Dehydration may not seem like a problem in a world of ice and snow but you lose more fluids to the surrounding dry air in the mountains than you do lower down. So it's vital to melt snow to provide you with an adequate water supply (you will need a minimum of four pints or two-and-a-half litres per day). Don't eat it however as this will reduce your core temperature and you will lose more calories melting it internally. It can also burn your mouth and give you painful blisters. Always carry a water bottle that you can stuff with snow. Hold it close to your body to melt it.

Finding food in the mountains can be more of a problem. Alpine crows and other birds do scavenge at altitude but they are extremely difficult to catch so your best bet is to head for the valleys lower down.

Come the morning, or better weather, you will need to continue your escape. (It is always handy to know which direction

**Above:** A Prusik Loop.

you're facing and your watch can help. If you're in the northern hemisphere, point the hour hand at the sun. Moving in an anticlockwise direction, halfway between the hour hand and twelve o'clock will be due south.)

Glaciers are another hazard that need to be overcome. Far from being a peaceful river of ice flowing slowly down a mountainside, glaciers are often criss-crossed with deep crevasses and ice caves that can be covered in thin layers of snow. They are extremely dangerous,

**Right:** Avalanche security equipment, including transceiver, probe and shovel.

even for the expert mountain guide. The safest way to negotiate a glacier is to be roped to a climbing partner so that one can arrest the fall of the other, but this is clearly not possible if you're alone. And in some cases, if one person falls, he or she may drag their climbing partners into the crevasse with them.

If you're climbing alone, it is often a good idea to drag your backpack behind you on a length of knotted rope. Should you fall into a crevasse or ice cave, the knots may dig into the snow and ice and, combined with the weight of the

backpack, help slow or even self-arrest the fall. Carry a spare length of cord in case you need to make a Prusik loop that will grip onto your main rope and help you climb out.

Although an ice cave might seem like a good place to shelter for the night, glaciers are unstable and can move up to 60 feet (18 metres) a day so the terrain is always shifting and collapsing. They should only be used as a last resort.

Some mountain gorges are spanned by the rope bridges of the mountain rescue teams but they need to be checked before you can cross. Protect your hands with gloves or by wrapping them in parts of your clothes, and then slide across (with a safety line made from your own rope) using a Tyrolean Traverse. This involves staying on the top rope with one foot hooked round it while the other leg hangs below to give you balance. You can then pull yourself across by the lower line if there are two. Maintaining your balance is crucial. If you slip off and end up underneath, you'll need to regain your position. Swing your right leg up and over the line, then your right shoulder. Then throw your left elbow over and swing back round. If you can't manage this, hook both feet over the top line and pull yourself to safety upside down.

If there are no rope bridges and you need to climb up or down a steep rock face, patience and planning usually pay off. Check the face carefully for the best route and then proceed slowly and methodically, keeping your hands at shoulder level so your arms don't tire quickly. Hand- and footholds need to be tested to assess whether they can take your weight, and you should try to maintain three points of contact at all times. Don't put all of your weight on

one hold; spread it between your hands and feet.

If there is no obvious way down, but you can see a glacial river below and believe it's deep enough, you may have to jump in. Only do this as a last resort if you absolutely have to cross the gorge. It's not safe to jump from more than about 50 feet (15 metres). Always jump feet first with your body vertical and your hands by your side. Then follow the instructions below on how to keep warm. (If you're lost in Iceland, for example, the landscape is dotted with geothermal pools that can keep you warm. Test the ground around the edge and the water / mud temperature first though – some of the volcanic vents are boiling, and others belch out toxic gases.)

Falling through ice into a lake is just another hazard of trekking in the mountains or polar regions. If you know you have no alternative and have to cross a lake, it's worth lighting a fire with any non-essential pieces of clothing or kit. Then, if you do fall in and manage to climb out, the heat from the fire could help save your life. Keep your centre of gravity low and spread your weight across your hands, chest and knees, and move slowly onto the ice. Keep your eyes and ears pealed for any noise or visible cracks. If you have a walking stick or ski pole, use it to probe the ice ahead. It needs to be at least three inches thick to support your weight. Ice is usually slightly thicker nearer the shore and can be thin towards the middle of the lake.

Should you happen to fall through, the initial immersion comes with its own hazards. The shock of the icy water is enough to cause your heart to race out of control and your breathing to come in panicked bursts. If you don't go into cardiac arrest and swallow a mouthful of water, you need to overcome the loss of coordination. The trick is to try remaining calm and controlling your breathing while dragging yourself out over the thicker ice from where you've come. You only have a short window of opportunity as blood will rush to your core to protect your vital organs. Your hands and feet will immediately lose their circulation so your coordination will suffer. Your larger muscle groups will cramp up within minutes and then you'll lose consciousness.

If you make it, remove all your clothes (you'll live longer naked than with your damp clothes sucking the last of your body heat) and roll in the snow to absorb any water clinging to your body. You can then try some vigorous exercises to force blood back into your extremities. Then wring out your clothes and revive yourself next to the fire.

If you make it down into the wooded valleys in the foothills, you should be able to find food. Ants' nests are common amongst the pine forests, and the larvae are particularly nutritious. Pine roots have a celery-like texture and contain important calories, and spring buds can also be found on the trees. Woodland snails are edible but you need to leave them for three days so that any poisons they've ingested have been purged from their systems. Dead fir trees are often home to beetles and other grubs, which are also nutrient-rich. In the cold, your body burns up twice as many calories just to maintain your core temperature, so food is a vital ingredient for survival. If you find plenty of grubs, take some with you but be careful to ration them for the long haul.

If you find a dead animal, check whether it's fresh. Mountain goats and chamois are edible providing the meat isn't rotting. If it is, you can eat the maggots feeding on the carcass. Bite off and discard the heads, but eat the bodies for their valuable protein. They can also be used for fish bait in the mountain rivers or night lines in the frozen lakes. Use any cord or cotton for the line, while any metal you have as part of your rucksack or clothing – in a bra, for example – can be fashioned into hooks.

Wrap the line around a rock, tie several hooks into it and attach the maggots, and then drop it into a hole in the ice. Stuff the hole with leaves and branches to prevent it refreezing, and then leave overnight. Any fish you catch can usually be eaten raw, although Old Man's Beard grows widely in alpine areas and tends to take a spark easily so cooking over an open fire shouldn't be a problem. Foxes and mountain rabbits can also be eaten but they need to be stalked and should be cooked because raw meat requires a lot of valuable energy to break down and digest. In Iceland, meat and fish can often be boiled in the volcanic vents.

The roots of the angelica plant are edible. The plant also contains a mild antibacterial agent that will help boost the immune system and can be used to clean your teeth.

Spruce trees on the south-facing valley walls (in the northern hemisphere they get the sun for longer and retain its heat) can be used to provide shelter in case you have to spend more nights on the mountain. Clear a platform beneath the tree by removing excess snow and then insulate the ground with pine fronds. More branches can be woven overhead to provide shelter from the elements. If your way out of the mountains involves more trekking through deep, soft snow, the spruce can also provide the basis for snow shoes.

Saplings can be bent into a tennis-racket shape and a couple of crossbeams can be added. When tied together with cord and attached to your boots, they should stop you sinking into the snow. Keep a large piece of wood in reserve in case anything breaks – it can also be used as a walking stick to steady you on uneven ground.

When making a fire, preparation is always the key. Have your tinder, kindling and bigger pieces of wood ready beforehand. Build a solid base to allow air to circulate and stack up snow behind the fire to reflect its heat in your direction. Then use your striker and flint to ignite the Old Man's Beard. A fire will provide welcome warmth at the end of the day

**Centre:** Andes survivors Fernando Parrado (L) and Roberto Canessa (R) with rescuer Sergio Catalan.

and allow you to melt snow for drinking water. Spruce or pine needle tea contains valuable Vitamin C and has been drunk by hunter-gatherers for thousands of years to ward off scurvy. (Pine needles also retain a lot of water so you can chew them if you're dehydrated.)

If you're using the fire to signal to potential rescuers, pile on as much living greenery as possible as this will create more smoke. This smoke can be seen for miles and it gives pilots clues about wind direction. As with all signal fires, you must make sure the tinder is bone dry because you need it to take a spark first time. It could mean the difference between life and death. With a little luck, it will lead rescuers to your position.

# Alive!

In October 1972, a plane carrying an amateur rugby team from Uruguay to Chile crashed in the Andes when the pilots misjudged their descent in poor weather. Miraculously, 33 of the 45 people on the flight survived the initial impact, although several more died from their injuries in the days that followed. Another eight perished when an avalanche struck the

wrecked fuselage two weeks later.

Their main problem was how to survive the intense cold at nearly 12,000 feet (3,700 metres). They packed the holes in the fuselage with suitcases and wore all of their clothes to keep warm. With search parties unable to find the plane, however, the survivors soon ran out of the little food and drink they'd

team-mates. At first, the thought of eating their friends and family seemed abhorrent, but, as they slowly starved (some even resorted to trying to eat the leather in their shoes, their clothes and the aircraft's upholstery) they began, as Roman Catholics, to look upon the meat as Holy Communion. In the end, they all resorted to anthropophagy, or the eating of human flesh for food. Although some may disagree, this differs from cannibalism in that the flesh is only eaten as an absolute necessity.

After more than two months, with their food running out and with no hope of rescue (they heard on the aircraft's radio that the search had been called off after only eight days), Nando Parrado and Roberto Canessa took the decision to try to find help. In an extraordinary survival story, the two men, both severely weakened by debilitating starvation and dehydration, and facing impossible odds, hiked for 10 days among the highest mountains in the world. They climbed several 15,000-foot (4,600m) peaks before they eventually came across a Chilean horseman who raised the alarm. Helicopters were dispatched to the site and the remaining survivors were finally rescued two days before Christmas.

packed. They solved the water problem by melting snow on the metal seatbacks, so the lack of food soon became their most pressing concern.

As there was no vegetation on the mountain, and they never saw any animals other than the odd bird, their thoughts soon turned to a ready supply of meat in the form of their dead

**Centre:** Jo
Simpson in front of
another terrifying
face - the North
Wall of the Eiger.

# Touching the Void

In 1985 Joe Simpson and climbing partner Simon Yates headed for the 20,800-foot (6,344-metre) Siula Grande in the Peruvian Andes. The pair successfully ascended the previously unclimbed west face of the mountain before making their way down the difficult north ridge in worsening weather.

Most mountaineering accidents happen on the descent and disaster struck when Simpson fell over a small ice cliff. The impact sent his tibia smashing through his knee joint into his femur. The pair appeared to be trapped in a storm several thousand feet above the glacier but they quickly rigged up a line so that Yates could lower his seriously injured partner down the face manually.

As night fell, Yates inadvertently lowered Simpson off a cliff. Unable to communicate with each other (they'd tied two 150-foot ropes together so they were 300 feet – 90 metres – apart) in the storm, Simpson couldn't tell Yates why he hadn't taken his weight off the rope. Yates couldn't move with Simpson's weight on it so they were effectively stranded. Just when they thought things couldn't get any worse, the snow seat that

Yates had dug to support them began to give way.

Yates was then faced with a difficult decision: try to maintain his position on the mountain, which would probably result in them both being pulled to their deaths when his seat gave way; or cut the rope. The latter might save his life but would condemn Simpson to death. He held on for as long as he could but, with frostbite and exposure threatening to overcome him, he pulled out a knife and cut the rope.

Yates was too exhausted to continue down in the appalling weather so he dug himself a snow cave and sheltered for the night. When he descended the following morning, he realised that

**Right:**
Shackleton.

**Far Right:**
Endurance locked in the polar ice cap.

Simpson had been hanging over a cliff above a deep crevasse. Stricken with grief, he tried to find Simpson's body but eventually gave up and returned to their camp eight kilometres (five miles) away.

Unbeknownst to Yates, Simpson had somehow survived his 150-foot (45-metre) fall into the crevasse and was lying semi-conscious on a small ledge. With no way of climbing out, he abseiled deeper into the ice gorge. By a stroke of tremendous good fortune, the bottom of the crevasse sloped steeply up to the edge of the glacier. With an enormous effort, and in terrible pain, Simpson eventually dragged himself out onto the glacier.

It took him another three days (with no food or water) to crawl back to the pair's camp. Exhausted and delirious, he finally made it to the tents as Yates was packing up to leave.

Arguments have raged ever since about Yates's decision to cut the rope. Many traditional mountaineers have savaged him for betraying his partner but, had he not cut the rope, he would have fallen 450 feet (140 metres) to almost certain death. Simpson, as we now know, would have survived his lesser fall, but there would have been no Yates to complete the rescue when he eventually crawled back to their camp. (The two had taken a friend along but, without Yates's insistence that they stay in the camp for a few extra days, he would probably have returned to civilisation sooner.)

Simpson has always defended

his partner and has gone on record saying he would have done the same. The moral and ethical issues will always remain but the simple fact is that Yates cut the rope and both men survived.

# Endurance

When Ernest Shackleton's ship *Endurance* became trapped in the ice of the Weddell Sea in 1915, the crew had no means of escape or of communicating with the outside world. He soon abandoned his plans to cross Antarctica on foot and set about ensuring that his men survived, which they did for the next two years (in the ship's hull) on a diet of seals and melted snow.

When the floes eventually crushed the ship, Shackleton led his team onto the ice. They built temporary shelters and hoped that the ice would drift to Paulet Island but progress was painfully slow and the ice soon began to break up. The team was left with no option but to take to the salvaged lifeboats and row for five days to Elephant Island beyond the

**Right:** Launch of the James Caird heading for South Georgia.

Antarctic peninsula. It was the first time they had stood on solid ground for 497 days. Realising that they were not going to be rescued because no one they were still alive, Shackleton set sail in one of the open 20-foot (six-metre) lifeboats for South Georgia 800 miles (1,300km) away, where there was a small whaling station. After more than two weeks, during which time they encountered icebergs and hurricane-force winds, the battered lifeboat finally reached South Georgia but they landed on the wrong side of the island.

Shackleton and his men had to climb the mountains down the island's spine (an expedition so dangerous that it wasn't replicated for 40 years) before they reached the whaling station and raised the alarm two days later. It would be another three months before the remaining men would be rescued from Elephant Island, however.

It had been an epic voyage across some of the most treacherous seas in the world, but Shackleton's unwavering belief had seen them emerge triumphantly from disaster.

**Centre:** The snowy wilderness.

# Surviving the Wilderness

Wilderness can take many forms: it can mean the mountains of Alaska, the dense forests of Eastern Europe, the icy wastes of Siberia, the swamps of Florida's Everglades, the barren Sierra Nevada or the parched outback of Australia, but the same basic survival principles apply: find shelter, water and food, and then look to be rescued. If you're stranded in the wilds of Alaska, however, you also need to be on the lookout for bears.

Brown and black bears are native to the foothills of the Alaskan mountains, and they are easily powerful enough to kill. Keep an eye out for trees that have had the bark stripped by their claws. It means you're entering dangerous country. Brown bears don't like being surprised, so it's important to make lots of noise. When they can hear you coming, they will usually avoid human contact. In a big group, making noise is easy – if you're on your own, it's best to call out every so often to let them know you're around. Local hunters are most at risk because they rely on slipping around silently and can often surprise the bears. Black bears, on the other hand, have been known to stalk human prey. Most natives carry guns for this reason. If you've made camp and have cooked any food, the bears can smell it from up to 20 miles away. If you have any food left over, always make sure you dispose of it a long way from your camp.

You need to react differently depending on which you come across. If it is a brown bear, the best course of action is to be submissive and back off slowly as it is likely to be defending its territory. Black bears are more likely to attack so you may have to fight it off.

Streams should almost always be followed as, aside from usually providing a source of fresh water, they often lead to rivers or lakes. Larger waterways are used by humans for travel and trade, so rescue is much more likely. However, you must avoid crossing fast-flowing glacial streams or rivers in the highlands as the cold water can be deadly if you're swept off your feet. Always try to cross at the shallowest point, which may not

**Above:** A pop ash tree being engulfed by a strangler fig.

is essential to keep your clothes dry as this may save your life when you reach the other side. Take them all off and stuff them into your backpack or waterproof jacket. Then throw it across to the other side or, if the water is only waist deep, wrap everything around your shoulders. Take a moment to prepare yourself mentally for the cold and then go for it, facing upstream into the current as it's better for balance.

You will have to move fast however, as the water in glacial streams will only be a degree or two above freezing. Relax your breathing to overcome the gasp reflex and get out the other side. Rub your body down vigorously with anything that will absorb the moisture and then pull your clothes on. Your hands and feet will need warm blood immediately if you're to avoid frostbite, so use anything to heat them up.

Rivers usually end up in the sea so, if you've been trekking in the wilderness, the coast will seem like a welcome change in scenery. In North America, these rivers are also likely to be packed with salmon, a great source of protein. But the bears will also be

be the narrowest. Wide, shallow riverbeds usually don't have the power to sweep you away, but deeper water in narrower courses can be more dangerous.

If you have no option and have to cross where it's deep and narrow, it attracted by an easy meal so you must keep an eye out for them. On the shore at low tide, food can be found in the shape of mussels and other shellfish. These and other crustaceans must always be properly cooked so the ability to make fire is essential.

Catching the fish is easiest with a spear, so you'll need to fashion one from a branch with your knife. Make sure you split and sharpen the ends into several points to give yourself the best chance of piercing the fish's skin. If you don't have a knife, try to drive the fish into the shallows and club them with a branch or rock. Again, patience is the key so approach from downstream and avoid casting your shadow across the fish or they'll think you're an eagle and bolt for deep water. If you get lucky, fresh salmon can be eaten raw. Berries and a plant known as Eskimo potato are plentiful in the forests of Alaska. The roots of the latter can be roasted or eaten raw. They are full of starchy carbohydrate and complement the fishy protein well.

Waterfalls are common in the mountains, so it pays to be vigilant. If you have to climb down alongside

**Above:** The deadly hemlock.

one, the first rules are to be patient and let your legs take the weight. There is always an eagerness to get down fast when climbing, but one mistake here could be your last so take your time, test each foot- and handhold first, and keep your bodyweight into the face.

# SURVIVING THE WILDERNESS

Spruce and alder forests cover much of lowland Alaska. Their wood can be useful for building a half-dome shelter, which is an easy and fast way to get out of the elements. Cut a number of 10-foot alder saplings and bend them into the shape of a bell before driving the ends into the ground. Thick spruce can then be used to cover and waterproof the dome. It also makes a good mattress.

If you're cold and wet after coming down off the mountainside, you'll need a fire to dry your clothes and stay warm. A fire is also good for keeping the spirits up, and a positive outlook is key to surviving in the wilderness. A flint is another essential piece of survival kit because it can be used to make embers when struck with a knife. Willow down makes good kindling but it is often damp so you'll need to persevere. It's best to have a supply of wood for the whole night as animals usually avoid fire.

Sleeping in the wilderness is never easy, particularly in extreme latitudes when it might be light for 20 hours each day, but sleep is almost as essential as food when it come to surviving. Indeed, most people will die from a lack of sleep before starving to death. Clearly this isn't a problem when shelter is available, but it would become an issue if you were stranded at sea where sleep wasn't possible.

A good night's sleep recharges the physical batteries and refreshes the mind, so it's vital for morale. A bad night can lead to overtiredness, poor decision-making and lower immunity to disease. In some parts of the world, like the Highlands of Scotland or the forests of Alaska, mosquitoes can be your biggest enemy at night. This is another reason why fire is so important as the smoke will discourage them from invading your camp. If you do get bitten, chew the leaves of the willow plant (they contain the ingredients found in aspirin) and rub the paste onto the bites.

Fire serves yet another purpose in that it is useful for signalling. Whether you're stranded in the desert, rainforest or icy wilderness, a signal fire can be seen for miles. In the coastal Alaskan wilderness in particular, evergreen foliage usually makes for white smoke that is even more visible against the dark backdrop of the forest. If you're sheltering in a cave, first check that

**Far Right:** The edible Eskimo Potato.

there are no predators lurking in its depths, and don't light a fire inside or you risk smoke inhalation and carbon monoxide poisoning. Light the fire in the entrance where there's plenty of ventilation and it will also keep bears and wolves at bay.

Travelling across frozen ground with supplies of food and water in a heavy backpack can be hard going. It's often a good idea to build a small sled to drag behind you. Small branches can be used for the runners, with crossbeams added for structural strength. The inside can be lined with animal fur if needs be. Using a length of rope wrapped around the waist or shoulders, it can then be dragged, leaving both hands free.

In difficult conditions it's always worth pacing yourself to limit sweat production. The more moisture on your exposed skin, the more heat you'll lose if it freezes. You should also continually set progress goals so that you break up a seemingly impossible journey into manageable chunks. This is good for morale and you'll feel like you're making real inroads. Surviving against the odds is about strength of mind as well as of body.

If you're stranded in a forest and the sun is obscured by cloud, it's easy to wander round in circles. If there's snow on the ground, check your tracks every 50 paces to make sure you're heading in the right direction. Of the five million hikers, climbers and rafters who visit the scorching lowlands, deep gorges and towering summits of the Sierra Nevada Mountains in California each year, two hundred end up in serious difficulty and need to be rescued.

If you are one of them, you should first look for water. Some of the alpine lakes are stagnant so you should try to find rainwater that has collected in depressions in the granite rocks. The mountains boast an abundance of obsidian and iron pyrite (fool's gold), but they will come in useful so you should keep any you find.

If you're stranded high up in the Sierra Nevada, you need to get down to the valley floors. Thunderstorms regularly roll in and you'll suffer from exposure at altitude. If you have to negotiate a steep rock face, always maintain friction with the rock via your hands and feet so you don't slide. False horizons are treacherous as you may end up climbing yourself further into difficulty.

If you reach the tree line, water and shelter should still be your priorities. If you don't have access to fire and can't boil water from the larger pools, carve out a small trench in any soft ground next to it. Any water that seeps into the trench will have been cleaned by the sandy soil and should then be safe to drink. If you are not sure about the quality of the water source, avoid drinking because you could ingest the giardia parasite that causes severe diarrhoea and dehydration and can put you out of action for weeks.

There are many rivers criss-crossing the Californian wilderness and it is usually a good idea to follow them as they should lead you to civilisation. If you need to make quick progress, it's worth hunting for driftwood and wild grape vines (which are also edible) to build a basic raft. Remember to build it close to the water's edge or you may not be able to drag it into the water. You should also keep your eyes and ears peeled for waterfalls and rapids as they can cascade through the canyons. Try to stay close to the shore at all times so you can get out of the water

**Centre:** Wild Salmon.

at short notice. If you get knocked off the raft, get out immediately and make a fire to dry your clothes and warm up.

If you're injured, keep an eye out for the yarrow plant as it contains powerful healing agents and can be rubbed into open wounds to sterilise them and help the blood coagulate. Look out for deadly hemlock, however, as it usually grows nearby. Indian potatoes are a great source of carbohydrate. Dig them out to find the juicy white bulbs. And the manzanita bush is usually a good source of berries that are rich in Vitamin C. The leaves are also good for cleaning your teeth as they act like a toothbrush.

Dead fir trees can be used to make the wiki shelters popular with Native American Indians. First make sure your camp doesn't have any game trails running through it, and then check for ants' nests. If the ground is clear, split the wood into strips and make a pyramid like a teepee. The frame can now be covered with pine fronds or more wood to insulate it from the cold of night.

In many parts of the world, squirrels, rabbits and small rodents are a good source of food, and they

can usually be caught with a simple snare. Use a shoelace or thin piece of cord or string and make a loop about two inches across, then tie it to a small branch or sharp stake and hang it over their tracks through the forest or scrubland (these tracks can often be seen with the naked eye, but animal droppings are another sign that you're in the right place). If the animal puts its head into the noose, it'll struggle and pull the cord tight, trapping itself for you to collect later. Don't set the snares too close to the animals' burrows as they are especially wary when leaving them.

It's best to set several traps and leave them overnight to give yourself the best chance of success. In a warm climate, you'll then need to skin and gut the animal before cooking. If it's cold, the animal may well have frozen and you'll need to cut fine shavings of meat before roasting. A rabbit will take about half an hour to cook over an open fire. In the Sierra Nevada, small water snakes can be eaten raw provided you remove the head. The indigenous people also used to fashion small cedar branches into deadly throwing sticks, but hitting deer or other animals takes plenty of practice. The cedar can also be shaved into tinder for a friction fire. Elder branches are best for this as they have a relatively low ignition point.

In the Tiger Forest of Siberia, shelter from the extreme cold is essential if you're going to survive several nights. Look for fallen branches to provide the backbone of a lean-to and wedge one end into a tree about four feet off the ground. Then use smaller branches as ribs for the framework and cover the ground with the thick sphagnum moss that exists throughout the forest. Cover the lot with several layers of pine fronds to keep your body heat inside. You'll then need to light a birch-bark fire (the bark contains flammable oils that light easily) to keep warm and ward off the wolves. The moss also contains iodine, which can be used to treat wounds as it acts like an antiseptic. Simply rub it into the affected area. Take some with you in case you need it later.

Elsewhere in the world, such as in the Scottish Highlands, the moss can be used as a water filter. If the ground is sodden, squeeze the moss to release the liquid. Otherwise strain any water through the moss to help remove dirt and purify it. When the moss rots it forms peat, which is a valuable fuel source because it burns like coal. Be very careful when crossing peat or marsh bogs, however. It's easy to fall in and difficult to get out. Fight the panic and try to keep calm, then use big, powerful strokes to head back the way you came because you know the ground there is solid. The moss can then be used to rub you down and remove any bacteria from animals rotting in the depths. Although it may be tempting to eat the mushrooms that grow amongst the moss, almost 80% are poisonous and they provide little nutritional value, so it's best to give them a wide berth.

Hunters in the Siberian wilderness often leave deer, boar, sable or reindeer carcasses when they've removed the meaty cuts. If they're fresh, the thick deer coats contain oils that make them waterproof. They can also provide warmth if you work fast, but removing them could take hours and cost you too much energy if they're frozen solid. You are still likely to be able to scavenge some meat left behind by the hunters because it is unlikely to spoil in the extreme cold.

**Centre:** A good knife is essential when traversing the wilderness.

They also occasionally slaughter yaks, which are another good source of food, and the thick hide can be used for clothing or bedding. The blood can be consumed fresh as it is crammed with vitamins and minerals. The nutrient-rich liver is considered a delicacy by the native Tuvans, and it can also be eaten raw. The eyeball is packed with protein and should also be eaten, although you will need a strong stomach to keep it down. Once you have eaten your fill, you should smear yourself with the animal's fat as it will keep out the worst of the cold.

The heat and humidity of Florida's Everglades is equally unforgiving and hundreds of tourists get lost here every year. If you lose your bearings, you'll need to be able to defend yourself should you be attacked by one of the million alligators. Find a sturdy branch and keep it with you. You can use it for self-defence and for probing the swamp in front of you. Try to make lots of noise so they know you're coming. If you surprise one, they're more likely to attack, but this may be preceded by a hissed warning that gives you time to back away safely. They tend to be more aggressive at dusk when they like to feed, and during the mating season. Make sure you've set up camp well before sundown so you don't run into any at night.

It's a good idea to build a platform of sturdy branches from the pop ash tree. It also has vines for lashing struts together. If you're on dry land, a simple A-frame shelter should suffice, although you need to make sure there are no ants' nests nearby. Use palm

it will still contain harmful bacteria and parasites so it will need to be boiled. There isn't much in the way of food but all the dead and rotting wood is usually home to a variety of edible grubs like carpenter ant larvae. And turtle meat is a valuable source of vitamins, minerals, salts and protein. You can also drink their blood. Cook them in their shells to lock in the flavour. Minnows in any pools can be eaten raw if you can catch them in a net made from your shirt.

If you're travelling by airboat and break down, it is usually best to stay with the machine because it's easier to spot. If you have not been rescued and need to move, it's always best to head for dry land. If you need to get your bearings, head for high ground. In the swamps, that means climbing a tree, which may be easier if you tie your shoelaces together to get better purchase on the bark. Palm trees grow on land, so head for them. If you can't see the wood for the trees, it's best to head west because the land is higher away from the coast. If you use the survival techniques listed here, you should be able to last long enough to be rescued.

fronds for bedding and then make a fire to keep the insects away. Tinder from the cabbage palm usually stays dry and will take a spark. Personal hygiene is perhaps most important in the swamps as you can end up with trench foot, so make sure you're clean and dry every evening. If you can't walk because your feet are rotting, you'll die.

Water from the swamps can be strained to remove dirt and debris but

# Six Weeks in the Wilderness

When Rita Chretien and husband Albert set off from British Columbia to Las Vegas in early 2011, they simply typed their destination into their van's GPS. Unfortunately, the GPS calculated the shortest route, which took them off the main road and through a remote and treacherous range of mountains. Neither they nor their vehicle were equipped for the trip. When their Chevrolet became bogged down in the mud, they decided to sit and wait for rescue, but, after three days, Albert struck out alone to find help. His body has never been found.

Rita survived in the van for 48 days on trail mix, boiled sweets and water from a nearby stream, although she lost more than two stone and was extremely weak when she was eventually found by local hunters.

The best advice when using GPS is to stick to main roads, don't put too much trust in it and use your common sense. If the terrain becomes unsuitable for your vehicle, plan an alternate route using major highways.

**Left:** Rita and Albert Chretien.

# Surviving the Rainforest

**Far Right:** Ants can be extremely poisonous and irritate your skin.

Rainforests cover about 15% of the earth's land surface and at least a million people visit the Amazon basin each year. From the mighty Andes in the west to the Atlantic Ocean in the east, the high-altitude cloud forest gradually gives way to the dense, humid jungle of the Amazon rainforest. This is an inhospitable place if you are not prepared, but, for the survivor, it can be a place of untold riches.

In the lush yet eerie cloud forests, the main dangers are exactly those you'd find in the world's mountain ranges: exposure, hypothermia and frostbite. So, priority number one is finding shelter or descending to a lower altitude where the vegetation is thicker and the cold isn't such a problem. Moving at an altitude of 10,000 feet (3,000 metres) saps the energy as there is 15% less oxygen than at sea level, so take time to rest and re-hydrate whenever possible. The heat and humidity will draw fluids from your body and you will need a bare minimum of 10 pints (six litres) per day. Water vines are a good source of fluid. Cut a seven-foot (two-metre) length and it will provide you with around a pint (half a litre).

It's usually a good idea to make some noise as you move through the jungle. This tells other animals

that you're coming and warns them to keep out of your way. If you're hungry, however, moving stealthily becomes a priority so you don't scare off lunch.

Finding food in the forest shouldn't be a problem: worms, small vine snakes, spiders, termites, grasshoppers, and palm weevil grubs that feed on the rotten wood are all on the menu, but watch out for jaguars, poisonous lizards and other venomous creepy-crawlies. Spear-nosed bats tend to keep to the caves carved out by small rivers and make a tasty snack, although they should be thoroughly cooked and you need to avoid being bitten as they can carry rabies. The

cave floors are likely to be covered in guano giving off toxic fumes and harbouring a host of spiders, scorpions and other biting insects. Caterpillars and ants should also be avoided as they can be extremely poisonous and irritate your skin.

If you need to hunt larger animals or fish, the local people make bows and arrows from the chonta palm because the wood splits lengthways and is extremely tough. Fibres from the leaves of the pita palm can be woven to make the drawstring. Piranhas are difficult to catch but are good to eat if cooked thoroughly to kill harmful parasites, although you need to make sure you aren't bleeding when you enter the water and there aren't hundreds of them because they will then attack and strip flesh from the bone with their razor-sharp teeth. Shallow pools in larger streams usually support small shoals. If you manage to spear one, wrap it in palm fronds and cook over the embers of a fire.

Termites can also be used to attract fish, although you will need a net to catch them. Bend a sapling into the shape of a tennis racket and then cover the frame with your shirt or trousers to use as the net itself (make sure you've tied the ends closed). Stand in a pool and sprinkle the termites on the water's surface while you hold the makeshift net underneath. If you're patient, the fish will soon swim above the net and you can pull them out of the water.

The indigenous population fashion blowpipes from bamboo and darts from the chonta palm. They then rub the tip of the dart across the back of a poisonous tree frog. The poison is so potent that it will shut down an animal's nervous system, but the kill will still be fine to eat. They have also developed a variety of deadweight traps that kill rodents by force when they try to remove the bait.

It's easy to get into trouble by misidentifying a plant. Leave all fungi well alone. Eighty percent are poisonous and even the experts make mistakes. The brown-spotted yellow orchid is easy to identify and edible, as is the fleshy red begonia. The flowers contain plenty of energy-giving glucose, while the leaves are packed with vitamins. Immature fern fronds with their familiar monkey tails are edible provided they have

**Far Left:** Cocoa beans in a cacao pod.

been boiled twice (to remove the coating of toxic slime), and they are a valuable source of food for the indigenous people. The ivory palm is also a staple of the native people, and it contains valuable carbohydrate. The fruit of the cacao tree is used to make chocolate and it is packed with vitamins and minerals. The seeds also release endorphins in the brain, giving you a morale boost.

Progress through the dense jungle is likely to be slow and you may be restricted to no more than a mile per day. It's also extremely easy to get disoriented and wander round in circles. If in doubt, head downhill and follow the streams because the going will be easier than battling through thick vegetation. They usually empty into the larger waterways used by humans, and that means rescue.

Beware of streams that are prone to flash floods and slopes that are prone to mudslides, however. Distant rainfall in the mountains can sometimes surge down narrow gullies and gorges, and the water level can rise in the blink of an eye. Debris and tide marks on the riverbanks will tell you if you're entering dangerous

**Right:** The brown-spotted yellow orchid.

terrain. If you need to cross one of these gullies but the slopes are too steep or look unstable, look out for trees that have fallen across them. Test them with your weight and then cross slowly in a sitting position using your arms and legs for balance.

If the going is relatively flat and there are no water courses, drag a long vine behind you to make sure you're travelling in a straight line. If there are no vines, mark a tree trunk or break a branch every 20 paces and try to keep them in line with one another. And if you can see the sun, you can always find a north/south line using the hour hand. If the terrain is steep and muddy, sharpen the end of a stick to use as a type of ice-axe to help your progress up and downhill.

You're likely to collect a number of cuts and bruises as you battle through the rainforest so keep an eye out for the heart-shaped leaves and smooth trunk of the dragon's blood tree, so called because its sap is red. This sap has antiseptic properties and can help prevent infection by ensuring blood

coagulates. Indeed, any open wound should be treated immediately as harmful bacteria thrive in the jungle. If they get into the wound, it'll quickly become infected. The leaves of the destroyer plant (with its little white flowers) can be crushed into an antiseptic paste and applied to the affected area.

Bamboo is common in the rainforests and its uses are virtually limitless: the chambers often store life-giving water; it can be used to make ladders for crossing streams or climbing sheer rock faces, and it

is usually strong enough to fashion into a raft should you need to travel downriver. Living vines can be used to lash the bamboo logs together.

The canopy provides reasonable shelter so your priority at night is to stay warm and dry, and, to do that, you'll need to be able to make fire. Finding dry tinder in the jungle may seem impossible but it can be found in the burrows of various animals or in the centre of dead branches. It rains most evenings in the cloud forests so make sure you collect your tinder,

**Far Right:**
Funghi.

kindling and larger logs, and then light your fire before dusk. If you have no flint, lighter or matches, it's probably not worth trying to make fire as the disappointment of failure will lower your morale.

If you don't have a fire, you are likely to be bitten by mosquitoes but you can do something to protect yourself. The reddish spoil from leaf cutter ants contains high concentrations of formic acid, which acts as a repellent, and it can be plastered over any exposed skin.

If you're desperate for a good night's sleep and need to build a shelter, make sure you start well before dusk and keep the bed above the ground so you aren't woken by the snakes, scorpions, insects and other animals on the forest floor. A hammock is one of the easier beds to make. Use two crosses of wood at each end and then weave vines into the hammock itself.

Personal hygiene may not be a top priority in a survival situation but it is vital if you're going to stay clear of disease, and washing in fresh rainwater is good for morale. It can also help you avoid the nasty botfly,

which likes to lay its eggs under your skin. The eggs incubate over about six weeks before the maggots erupt from the thumb-sized lump in your flesh. A wash and a rest will also help you recharge your batteries, so you'll be able to cover more ground later.

If you're lost and not making enough progress, use the rivers as a last resort. They flow quickly and you'll cover a lot more ground, but they can also be dangerous so it pays to be vigilant. In rapids, keep your legs in front of you to protect against larger rocks. If you have the time and resources to build a bamboo or balsa raft first, you should do so. Piranhas and other nasty fish like slow-moving water so keep your limbs in the raft at all times.

If there are no rivers and you're completely lost, head for high ground and build a signal fire to attract attention. If you can't find a clearing in the jungle, build your fire under the biggest break in the tree canopy. The air in the rainforests is usually still so the smoke should rise above the canopy, and it will be visible for miles if you burn fresh greenery that smokes. If you're lucky, your fire will be seen and you'll be rescued.

# SURVIVING THE RAINFOREST

**Right:** Yossi Ghinsberg.

**Above:** Amazon rainforest.

# More Dead than Alive

In 1981, Israeli-born Yossi Ghinsberg headed into the depths of the Bolivian rainforest with three companions, Marcus, Kevin, and guide Karl to hunt for lost villages and undiscovered tribes. They were poorly equipped and were soon hopelessly lost themselves, and it appeared that neither the villages nor the tribes actually existed. They split up but Marcus succumbed to a flesh-eating fungus and Karl was never seen again.

With their condition worsening and with no hope of rescue, Ghinsberg and Kevin built a raft and floated downriver but, as they approached a waterfall, they lost control. Kevin managed to scramble ashore but Ghinsberg was thrown over and then endured 20 minutes in fearsome rapids. Despite trying to find Kevin, he soon gave up. For the next 19 days, Ghinsberg survived alone, his unfailing belief helping him remain positive. He ate very little food apart from the odd piece of fruit and a few raw birds' eggs but the heavy rains provided him with plenty of water. Having survived an encounter with a jaguar by improvising a flame-thrower with a can of insect repellent and a lighter, he began to feel more confident that he would survive. This confidence was short-lived. He almost died in a flood and then got caught in a bog. When he eventually freed himself his feet were in such a state that he could no longer walk.

Kevin was eventually rescued so he helped organise a search party. Somewhat incredibly, they found Ghinsberg unconscious on the riverbank. It took him almost six months to recover because he had picked up several infections and was in appalling physical condition.

**Centre:** The dragon's blood tree.

# Surviving the African Bush

The African bush, plains and savannah may look like the ideal safari destination but getting lost is all too easy and some of the general rules of survival that apply elsewhere are not recommended here. For example, using the rivers to cover a lot of ground in the African jungle is not always the best option. Although fast-flowing water and rapids are usually safe, beware the wider, shallower rivers that meander through the forests or across the savannah. Hippos and crocodiles kill more people than any of the big game animals like lions and buffalo. Hippos don't like being surprised and can get very aggressive if you block their route to water. They have also been known to attack and overturn small boats that encroach on their territory or get too close to their young.

Crocodiles are ambush killers that lie in wait just below the water's surface. When animals come to drink, they propel themselves out of the water with their powerful tails and snatch prey items in their huge jaws. They will then drag the animal into deep water to drown it before tearing off chunks of flesh with a flick of their heads or a roll of their massive bodies. For this reason, never drink from the same spot on the bank, and only fish from the water's

**Above:** The fearsome rhino beetle.

**Centre:** Crocodiles.

edge as a last resort. The croc will watch you the first time and attack the second. If you get taken, your only hope of survival is to gouge its eyes or ram an arm deeper into its mouth to force its gullet open. If the croc begins to swallow water, it may release you.

The heat and humidity of the African jungle is also a killer, albeit a slower one. Progress through the dense vegetation is likely to be slow, with bushes of spiked camel and buffalo horn tearing into your flesh like razor wire. If you make it into the open bush-land, the humidity will become your greatest enemy. In extreme conditions, you can lose up to 12 litres of fluid in a day, or around 14% of your bodyweight. A two or

three percent fall in bodyweight due to fluid loss means you're dehydrated, so you can expect cramps, nausea, exhaustion and heatstroke. If you don't re-hydrate, your physical and mental condition will deteriorate rapidly. Stay in the shade and drink as much fluid as you can.

Water from the rivers must be boiled first, but you can drink dew if you know how to collect it. You should always be on the move early in the morning to avoid the blistering heat of the day, so there may still be dew on the long grass. Remove your shirt and tie it round one leg. As you walk, the dew will be absorbed by the shirt and can then be wrung out as fresh water. In the rainy season, collecting fluid shouldn't

be a problem, but it does mean the animals will move further from their water source at the river and could surprise you at any moment.

Elephants are extremely protective of their young and will attack to defend the herd. No other animal in Africa will attack you in a vehicle but elephants will, so it is vital not to surprise them. If they flap their ears and grunt at you, move away slowly and try to get downwind so they can't smell you. Their eyesight is poor so you should then be able to back off safely. If they flatten their ears against their bodies and curl their trunks, they could be about to charge. If this happens, it is supposed to be better to stand your ground because they can easily outrun you over uneven terrain, but facing down an angry eight-ton matriarch could easily end in a trampling. If you run, make sharp turns to confuse it and it may lose you.

Buffalo and rhino can also become aggressive if disturbed. Rhino will tend to take up a defensive position to check you out. Their eyesight is also poor but they have a keen sense of smell and will charge if you get too

close. As with an elephant charge, the best thing to do is face it down. If the animal keeps on coming, dive to one side at the last minute and then break for cover.

In the bush you need to keep your eyes and ears on full alert. If you can hear birds chirping and other noise, this is a good sign. If everything goes quiet, it's likely that predators are around and you will need to take extra care. Baboons act as a good early-warning system because they will make a racket if they spot a leopard. If you're lost and have to shelter for the night, stay close to the troop as, apart from sounding a warning, they also tend to sleep near a fresh-water source.

Sleeping near the water brings its own hazards, however, as malaria-carrying mosquitoes love the humidity. Malaria kills a million Africans every year so you must avoid being bitten if possible. Burning blackjack plants (which are also edible if you're desperate for food) acts as a natural insecticide and should keep them away, and the fire will also deter other predators. In the morning, put your fire out and leave

**Far Left:** An acacia tree.

**Right:** The edible blackjack plant has a number of uses.

a marker pointing in the direction you're travelling so that if anyone finds your camp they'll know where you are.

Leopard tracks are quite distinctive with three forward pads. They also retract their claws when they're on the move so they don't make indents in the ground. If you have no other option, you can follow the tracks in the hope that they lead to the remains of its kill, but you will need to be on the lookout for other scavengers like lions and hyenas.

Although there have been several cases in the past, hyenas are unlikely to attack a healthy human, but lions will. They are ambush and chase predators, so the worst thing you can do is run as that only ignites their hunting instinct. If you are attacked, stand tall, wave your arms and make as much noise as possible. If you're lucky, they'll back off.

Circling vultures are another sign that there's a fresh kill on the ground (they will only eat fresh meat). If you're starving, you may have to find the carcass, but other animals will do the same. If there are no maggots and the kill doesn't smell rotten, it

has probably been made recently and the meat under the skin that hasn't drawn flies or been scavenged already should be good to eat.

Locals get plenty of bush food from the acacia tree. They listen to the bark for rhino beetle larvae and other grubs, before peeling it back and removing them. They are best served cooked but can be eaten raw if necessary. They also hunt giant African bullfrogs. They are edible but they will secrete a poison if approached and have large front teeth so need to be handled with care. A swift strike with a knife should finish it. The meat should be cooked, but you'll need to avoid the skin. The mopane tree is usually covered with edible worms and is another valuable source of food. Take the worms by the head and squeeze the guts out, then make sure you cook them to burn off the irritant hairs. Scorpions can also be eaten once the stinger has been removed, and you can also remove the pincers to avoid getting bitten.

If you eat something that doesn't agree with you, dehydration again becomes your biggest enemy – you can lose up to 40 times more fluid than normal. You will also lose valuable salts and minerals that have to be replaced if you're going to survive. Make sure you're always carrying charcoal from a previous fire. It can be crammed into a spare pocket from your backpack or even a sock. The charcoal will absorb toxins and filter the water, and it can then be strained before being boiled. This should help combat the harmful bacteria in your gut. You can mix in a little crushed charcoal to be sure of getting its benefits. If you can't make a fire, strain the water through the charcoal several times.

Baobab trees may seem like a good place to shelter as they can be hollow, but they are often used by other predators and are usually home to voracious black or soldier ants, snakes and scorpions. It is often a better idea to climb into the crook of the tree and make camp off the ground. The fruit from the tree is one of the African staples and it's crammed with Vitamin C.

You need to give yourself enough time to make camp before the sun goes down. If you hold your hand out towards the sun and spread your fingers vertically, the distance between each digit is about 15 minutes, so if the sun is two fingers above the horizon you've got about half an hour before it sets.

If you are stranded further north in Africa, the midday heat is usually drier, but equally oppressive and dangerous. The animals, too, are just as likely to attack if they are cornered, surprised, or feel you are threatening their young, so it always pays to tune into your surroundings and remain vigilant.

If you are on safari and your vehicle breaks down, it is almost always best to stay with it. If you head out across the savannah alone, you risk animal attack, disorientation and dehydration. The vehicle will also be much easier to spot from the air and the ground. If you get lost on a walking safari, you are putting yourself in danger of animal attacks, and man-eating lions are known to live in the Kenyan game reserves.

If you have no vehicle and decide to escape on foot, pick a distant landmark and head for it. Even near the equator, mountains can be a good source of fresh water, but you could also head for a distant river as humans use them for travel and trade. However, unlike in most parts of the world, it is not always the best option to follow small rivers downstream as they can suddenly vanish into underground aquifers. Sometimes it's better to head upstream to search for civilisation near the source.

Heading for high ground is also a good idea because you can assess the layout of the land and see much further. Animal trails are often visible from a distance and they can lead to water. Even dry riverbeds can provide water but you'll need to avoid the stagnant water in pools as it contains harmful bacteria and parasites and is undrinkable. If you are left with no option, you can squeeze some water from fresh elephant dung, although this too can contain unpleasant bacteria.

Dry riverbeds are often lined with caves that only become visible in the dry season. If other animals have used the cave for shelter, line the entrance with thorny acacia branches to deter them from returning. If you do get surprised, make sure you can defend yourself. A simple spear can be made by tying your knife to the end of a thin branch. The inside of a cave can be up to 20 degrees cooler than the savannah so they can be good places to rest during the heat of the day. If you have no water, walking at dusk and early in the morning will allow you to last twice as long than if you walk during the midday heat.

If you have no choice but to move at night when the African predators are most active, you can get a bearing from the moon as it also rises in the east and sets in the west. Use all of your senses to warn you of predators.

If you have to climb a rocky outcrop or cross open grassland, look out for puff adders. They won't move out of your way and will strike if approached. If you get bitten and don't have anti-venom, you will probably die within 24 hours. Give them a wide berth at all times.

As you progress through the bush, you'll realise that all life in Africa is locked in a struggle for survival. Like our ancestors, if you want to get out alive, you must learn to use your brain to understand the animals and overcome the three main obstacles: finding shelter, water and food.

# Surviving the Outback

The outback can take one of many forms, whether it's the canyons of Central America, the barren bush in Australia or the steppes of Asia. Australia is a country of extremes. It covers an area of nearly three million square miles (7.7 million km²), has maximum temperatures that reach 57°C (134°F), and is home to some of the most deadly animals on the planet (21 of the world's 25 most venomous snakes live here). Five million visitors come to the outback every year but hundreds need rescuing from the brutal landscape, and around 40 will die from the heat, snakebites or getting caught in a tropical cyclone.

In the Kimberley in north-western Australia (an area the size of California) there are only 30,000 people, most of whom live on the coast. In this sparsely populated area of sandstone cliffs, vast scrub deserts and deep gorges with dry riverbeds, you'll need to rely on your wits and knowledge to survive and make your way to safety. For eight months of the year there is no rain at all, although surviving in the oppressive heat and humidity of the wet season can be even tougher. If you get lost and have no survival skills, there's a 75% chance you'll be dead within a week.

If you do lose your way, head for high ground to assess your situation. There's only one road across this vast

**Left:** Seed pods on the kapok tree.

landscape, so you're unlikely to be rescued immediately. But if you'd studied a map beforehand, you'd know that the highway runs to the south and there are a few small settlements on the coast to the northwest. You can get a bearing in the southern hemisphere by pointing twelve o'clock on your watch at the sun. Then, moving in a clockwise direction, halfway between the hour hand and twelve o'clock is due north. Once you've made up your mind which to head for – the coast or the road – stick with your decision.

In ancient times the aboriginal people survived here and it's their skills you'll need if you're going to find your way back to civilisation. They quickly learned to respect the land and the scorching heat. Try not to

# SURVIVING THE OUTBACK

walk too far and look for shade instead during the heat of the day. It can be 30 degrees cooler and could save your life. The humidity in the outback can be 100%, which means your sweat cannot evaporate and cool you down. If you continue in direct sunlight, you'll suffer heatstroke and dehydration, both of which can be fatal. Use any part of your pack or clothing to cover your head as your brain must be kept cool.

It's not ideal but, if you can't find a water source, in an emergency you can drink your own urine. It's 95% pure water and sterile when fresh, so you need to drink it immediately. As you'll need two pints (1.25 litres) of water per hour, however, it's not a long-term solution.

In the wet season, tropical storms can suddenly sweep across the landscape. You may well need a fire to overcome the cold of the night, so collect your tinder before dusk when it's still dry. The seed pods from the kapok tree contain a cotton wool-like substance that will easily take a spark.

As the weather closes in, you'll need to make camp. Choose your location carefully as flash floods can sweep through dry riverbeds. Keep your

platform off the ground but away from tall trees as lightning during storms in the Kimberley can be quite intense. Wooden struts can be used for a makeshift shelter and bed, ivy for rope, and eucalyptus leaves and bracken for cover and a mattress. If it does rain, always fill your water bottle and have a wash. And make sure the roof of your shelter slopes away from your head so the water runs off.

If you've managed to build a shelter and have a temporary water supply, your next priority is food. The fruit of rock fig trees can provide valuable fuel and Vitamin C but they are usually high up in the branches. Its roots bed deep in the rock so they should be safe to use as handholds. The wallaroo bush's sweet white berries are also edible. Protein can be found in the form of spiders, insects and other small grubs. Spider webs can also be bundled up and inserted into wounds as a primitive field dressing.

If you're on the move, you simply can't carry enough water to get very far, so you'll need to find another source. Even heavy overnight rains will evaporate by the following afternoon so your best bet is to look

for a narrow gorge or gulley that might still have rainwater at the bottom. If possible, always check where the water is coming from because a stagnant pool might be full of harmful bacteria. If the source is an underground spring or it has filtered through the rock and sand, it shouldn't need to be boiled and will be safe to drink. Make a mental note of where these water sources are in case you have to come back to them.

You should break down the day into manageable chunks so that you can achieve your goals before moving on. Try walking for an hour and then resting for 10 minutes. Every time you take a breather, you'll feel better and maintain your morale. At the core of every survival story is a person who refused to give up and stayed mentally strong. Half the battle is always psychological.

As is usually the case, small streams lead to bigger waterways, so they should be followed. In the Kimberley, the rivers all lead to the north coast of Australia and people always cluster near the ocean. As the waterways increase in size, however, you need to keep an eye out for crocodiles. The freshwater crocs (identified by their long, thin snouts) are more docile and are usually smaller, but they will still attack if cornered or surprised. Saltwater crocodiles are much larger and extremely aggressive during their breeding season. They can only be sustained in areas where there are plenty of prey items like large fish and animals that feed along the banks, but unwary humans have been attacked even in smaller pools. With a bite force of one-tonne per square-inch, your chances of surviving are virtually zero.

If you manage to give the crocs a wide berth, you should keep with the water course until you reach civilisation and rescue. If you've mastered sourcing food and water but you headed for the road, you should be able to last long enough to attract a passing motorist.

# Left for Dead

In 2006, Ricky Megee was kidnapped on the Buntine Highway before being drugged and left for dead in the inhospitable outback of Northern Australia. He had no food, water, shoes or a vehicle, and was stranded in the blistering heat. He walked for 10 days before coming across a dam.

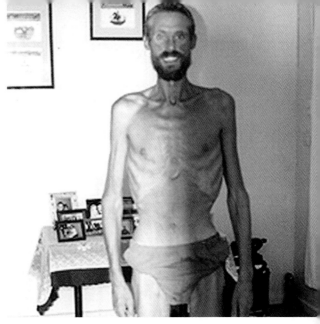

He had no idea how to survive and knew he wouldn't last if he left the area so he set up camp and lived on frogs, leeches, grasshoppers and a few plants. Over the next two-and-a-half months, Megee lost 130 pounds (60kg) in bodyweight.

He eventually decided that he had to walk to safety and struck out across the unforgiving outback. Several days later, farm manager Mark Clifford found the 35-year-old in a terrible state. Although some doubt has been thrown on his

**Above:** Ricky Megee was lucky to have survived severe malnutrition in the outback.

**Far Left:** A rock fig tree.

**Centre:** Making a bamboo fire saw.

that direction (again, it always pays to know the area you're entering as these small slivers of information may help save you).

At more than 9,000 feet (2,700 metres) above sea level, the days may be hot under relentless sunshine but the nights can be bitterly cold. If you are stranded on a ridge at the top of the system, you will need to descend before nightfall so you don't freeze to death when the temperature falls to -10°C (14°F). The canyon is over a mile (1.5km) deep so you need to take extreme care when making your way to the valley floor. Look for lines of weakness in the rocks as they can provide the hand- and footholds you'll need to climb down.

Down-climbing is almost always more dangerous than scaling a cliff as you constantly have to lean out to plan your descent. You also can't see the holds as you come to them, and you may end up getting stuck with no way of climbing up or down. Where rock overhangs, you may have to descend blindly. Beware loose and crumbling rocks as they might give way. They also might be home to scorpions and tarantulas. The former can be eaten raw if you remove the stinger; the latter should be cooked as the hairs on their abdomens are an irritant and can be fired at a predator when the spider feels threatened. Edible beetle larvae can often be found in the scrub.

If you make it to the canyon floor,

(making sure the lower piece is held firmly in place with rocks). Yucca has a low ignition temperature so you should be able to create an ember, but, as with all techniques for making fire, you'll need to be patient. Preparation is also the key: remember to collect your tinder, kindling and wood first, and be ready well before nightfall.

If you're still lost in the morning and need to take another bearing, you can use a sliver of metal from your backpack to make a rudimentary compass. Fill a small depression in the rock with water and then magnetise the metal by rubbing it in your hair. Lay it gently on a leaf floating on the surface tension and it should swing round to give you a north/south line. If you know where the sun rose, you have all four points of the compass.

In these canyon systems and elsewhere in the world where indigenous populations still live, you should see signs of their camps and trails. The tracks will invariably lead to water running along the base of the gorge, and it will also be much warmer as the canyon walls act like a suntrap. Once at the bottom, however, you will be forced to follow the system, so you

look to shelter for the night in a cave and make a fire. If you don't have an immediate source of flame, you can use the abundant yucca plants to make a fire saw. Remove the base and split the wood into strips. Then saw one piece across the other above your tinder

**Above:** Waterfall.

**Centre:** The Chihuahua-Pacific Railway.

**Far Right:** Aboriginal Australian.

distant rumbling like a jet aircraft, or feel the ground begin to tremble, head immediately for higher ground.

Canyons often contain waterfalls. You should avoid them as they are dangerous, but if they block the route you need to take and you can't climb round, you may need to jump. You must gauge the height accurately because you'll need the water at the base to be half as deep (if you jump from 33 feet or 10 metres, the water will need to be 16 feet deep). Yucca leaves can be torn into strips and used as string. Tie several lengths together and then wrap one end around a rock. This primitive depth gauge can then

need to make sure you're still heading in the right direction. If the river starts taking you away from your goal, look for tributaries or other gorges that follow your initial course.

Once again, beware of signs of flash flooding: debris such as trees, branches and other detritus, or an obvious tidemark higher than the current water level. Although the weather may be fine where you are, it could be raining heavily 30 miles away. If you hear a

LITTLE BOOK OF **OUTDOOR SURVIVAL**

be used to sound the pool beneath the waterfall. When the rock is on the bottom, pull it out an arm-length (three feet or one metre) at a time and wait for it to break the surface. If the water is deep enough, jump feet first with your legs together and your arms by your sides.

If the current takes you, the best way to make it back to the shore is to corkscrew with one front crawl stroke followed by one backstroke. If the water is cold, you'll need to make a fire to dry your clothes. The native people often dig a shallow trench and line the bottom with cypress branches for comfort, and then light a small

**Far Right:** Aron Ralston.

fire on either side to keep themselves warm overnight.

You may have a ready source of water but you'll still need food and the river can provide it. Trout and other edible species (all freshwater fish are safe to eat) can be found in the waterway but, if you have no rod or line, you'll need to dam a small tributary to trap the fish. Choose a shallow section and use any rocks to block the downstream end first. Try to stay out of sight as you dam the upstream end 30 yards away or the fish will sense you and try to escape. Then circle back round behind them and try to bludgeon them with a large stick. Even if you miss, the shockwave should concuss them.

Remove the head and tail with your knife, and then wash the guts out in the river. If you haven't got time to make a fire, this protein-rich meat can be eaten raw. A good feed helps boost the immune system, delivers valuable oils and raises morale.

Now that you can provide shelter, water and food, and you have mastered making fire, you should be able to survive for the long haul. Keep taking bearings and following the canyon system until you reach safety or are rescued.

# Between a Rock and a Hard Place

In April 2003, young adventurer Aron Ralston had his arm trapped by a falling boulder in the Blue John Canyon in Utah. Somewhat foolishly he hadn't told anyone his plans so he knew he wouldn't be missed. With no one searching for him, he rationed what little water he had and tried to free his arm. It was no use because the boulder weighed approximately 800 pounds (360kg).

Dehydrated and delirious, Ralston eventually decided to break his arm and then amputate it using a small blunt multi-tool. It took him about an hour and he lost a quarter of his overall blood volume. He then had to climb out of the canyon and rappel down a small cliff. He was eventually rescued by a family after five days, during which time he lost 40 pounds (18kg) in weight.

kidnapping story (he also claimed his car had broken down, and he had minor drug offences to his name), there is no disputing the fact that he survived in some of the most extreme conditions on earth for 10 weeks.

The canyons of Central America can be equally inhospitable. Three hundred miles from the American border, Mexico's Copper Canyon system is four times larger and a 1,000 feet (300 metres) deeper than the Grand Canyon.

Because of its breathtaking scenery, half a million people now visit the area each year, but many are ill-equipped to deal with the barren landscape. As many of the gorges still haven't been mapped, hikers who get lost without a guide can quickly find themselves in serious trouble.

It's relatively easy to get a compass bearing in the canyons. Being north of the equator, the northern side of the valley receives less sunlight and therefore retains its moisture (so it's covered in vegetation), while the other is parched and not as lush and faces south. The Chihuahua-Pacific railway line runs to the west of the canyon system, so you should head in

**Left:** Saltwater Crocodile.

# Surviving the Desert

When people think of the desert, one place usually springs to mind: the Sahara in North Africa, a three-and-a-half-million-square-mile cauldron of unforgiving heat, immense sand dunes and precious little in the way of life. There are many other deserts around the world, but the hardest one to survive is the Sahara. If you're stranded out here without water, you'll be dead in less than two days.

Your biggest enemies are by now familiar – dehydration and heatstroke – so finding water is your immediate priority. Heatstroke can come on in an hour or so and is characterised by a headache and general lethargy. If you don't find shade, your body will eventually stop sweating to conserve vital fluids. If you can't sweat, you can't cool down, and that leads to a quick death. Dehydration can creep up on you but is equally deadly.

The desert is so large that, unless you're at its edge, you'll have no hope of making it to the Atlas Mountains, Mediterranean, jungles of the Congo or the Nile. You need to stay alive long enough to be found by rescuers or the nomadic tribesmen who still wander the unforgiving landscape.

Always cover your head, and pee on your hat if necessary to keep it cool; then head for high ground to gauge the lie of the land. The

**Above:** Making a friction fire.

**Centre:** The highly toxic Calotropis plant.

sand on the dunes can be deep and going will be hard so try to keep to the ridges rather than climbing the face directly. Shrubs and trees need water, so it's often a good idea to head for any greenery. The hunt for water always involves balancing risk versus reward, however. If you know there's a small water source five miles away, you have to know how much sweat you'll lose getting there. That distance could take several hours to cover if there are dunes to cross and, in the fierce heat of the day, you can lose three pints of fluid (two litres) per hour. After just a couple of hours you'll be moderately dehydrated, your decision making and coordination will suffer, and from there things can go downhill rapidly.

Depressions in dry riverbeds are a good place to search for water as the pools evaporate slowly. If you dig in the sand you might get lucky. Squeeze and strain the darker soil through your T-shirt to extract any moisture. If there's not enough to live on, you may be forced to drink your own urine, although this should be a last resort. The water you do have should be kept in the mouth for as long as possible to keep your

**Above:** The Dollar Plant.

throat moist.

You will need to eat to keep your strength and your spirits up, and camel spiders are a good source of protein. They're aggressive and can give you a nasty nip so remove the head and only eat the abdomen. You should eat little and often rather than feasting as a big meal requires a lot of water to aid digestion. Fat-tailed scorpions are another food source but you'll need to remove the stinger and head as they are among the most venomous in the world. If you get bitten or stung, try to find the desert gourd as its fruit has antiseptic and anti-inflammatory properties. Don't eat the fruit though: it's bitter and will upset your stomach, causing dehydration. Sand lizards can be eaten, but they are difficult to catch. Sand beetles don't taste great but can also be eaten. They provide protein and valuable salts, as do little Saharan frogs.

Palm trees can be a godsend. They provide shade, which can be 30 degrees cooler than the surrounding area, and they can also be a source of food (dates) and water. You may have to monkey climb the palm to reach the dates, so take it slowly and stay

patient. Dates contain lots of sugar, minerals and Vitamin C, so you should make every effort to harvest them. Fill your backpack if necessary as they won't spoil immediately. Digging a shallow trench in the shade of the tree can also be a good idea. The sand below the surface can be up to 60 degrees cooler.

If digging at the base of the palm doesn't lead to water, you can try making a dew trap. Dig out a depression several feet (one metre) across and around a foot (30cm) deep. Line it with palm leaves and then place a few rocks on top. As the rocks cool overnight before warming in the morning sun, the contrast allows condensation to form on their surface. Cover the lot with more palm leaves to prevent evaporation, and you may get a few precious drops.

It's a good idea to make camp under the palms but sand is a terrible insulator. In the bitter cold of the desert night (there are no clouds to trap the warmth of the day) you'll need to stay warm by making a palm-frond mattress and then lighting a friction fire using a spindle and wooden

**Left:** A sand lizard.

base. As you rotate the spindle into a knot in the base, friction will cause the wood to heat up and eventually you should get an ember. The trick is not to rush the early stages and to be patient. Don't be disheartened if it doesn't work, and don't try too hard if it means losing yet more sweat. You'll be better off covering yourself in palm fronds to keep warm.

It's best to move early in the day before the sun's heat incapacitates you. Be careful pulling on boots and hats as scorpions are nocturnal and might have crawled inside. If you made a fire the night before, rub some of the charcoal into your cheeks to cut out the glare. Never remove your shirt because sunburn can be deadly. You'll also need to keep an eye out for snakes, the cobra and horned viper in particular. If you come across one, back away slowly to give it room. They're more likely to strike if cornered. The vipers can burrow into the sand and are easily trodden on so you must watch your step. Their haemotoxic venom can

**Left:** Every part of the oleander shrub is toxic so it should be avoided. It can also pollute local water sources.

cause severe internal haemorrhaging and lead to a heart attack, so, if you're bitten on a finger or toe and have no way of reaching a hospital with anti-venom, you may have to amputate immediately. They are edible however, so if you're starving, you may have to kill one. Remove the head, skin and guts, and roast over a fire.

It's not only the animals that can do you harm. The calotropis plant has beguiling fruit that look like avocado but give it a wide berth. The sap is highly toxic and the fruit can give you severe diarrhoea. As a general

**Right:** Beware the deadly Horned Viper.

rule, any plant with a white, milky sap should be avoided. This is also true for the euphorbia, which looks like a cactus. If the sap gets onto your skin it causes extreme irritation, and it can blind you if it gets into your eyes.

Many rivers in the Sahara run deep underground but water does occasionally bubble to the surface. It usually only turns the sand into a deadly trap, however. If you fall into quicksand, you need to try to raise you legs and spread your bodyweight. Don't struggle as this will only sap your energy and draw you further in, so you need to control your breathing and remain calm. You shouldn't be able to sink as the sand is denser than you but if you can't get out you'll be killed by the relentless sun. Once you've raised your legs, try to slide across the surface to safety. You'll then need to remove the mud from your clothes or it'll give you sores when you start to walk.

It is often a good idea only to move at night, and you could double the distance you travel, but you'll need to be aware that most of the desert's creep-crawlies are nocturnal.

**Far Right:** Desert Gourd.

If you are walking by night, make some noise so that the creatures know you're coming and have time to get out of your way. It may be much colder at night but you'll soon warm up by covering a lot of ground. You'll need to rest during the day, and, for that to be of any benefit, you'll have to find shade as soon as the sun comes up. Always plan ahead if possible.

Sandstorms can be triggered by the heat and the best place to ride one out is on the desert floor. The quickest way down a dune is to run, but lean back and take big strides to avoid falling. It's easy to get lost and overpowered by a storm so lie down on the ground and cover your mouth to avoid inhaling the stand.

Finding a bearing in the desert can be accomplished with your watch (as described earlier) but the prevailing sirocco wind off the Mediterranean also helps by sculpting the dunes. The shallow windward side will usually be to the north, while the leeward side will usually face south. If you're walking at night, the North Star can be found by tracing a line from the last two stars in the Big Dipper, although it's four times higher in the sky.

Much of the Sahara is barren rock and looks more like the surface of Mars. The odd acacia tree can be found, and the gum on its branches can be chewed to get the saliva flowing. They are also a sign that you might be closer to the Atlas Mountains. The Berber people have lived and hunted in this region for thousands of years and they may be your only hope of rescue. They have a mental map of all the wells because they rely on water for their survival.

In this part of Morocco, French is the language of these nomadic peoples. They often have goats and camels, both of which can save your life. Camel's milk is rich in Vitamin C and iron, and goats provide valuable meat. When a camel gets old, they put it out of its misery quickly and then use almost every part of it for food, water and shelter. The skin can be used as a blanket, and the fat in the hump is considered a delicacy. The stomach is divided into three parts, one of which, the rumen, filters out the fluids and is a great source of water. The camel's partially digested

food can also be strained, although you'll need a strong stomach to keep the fluid down.

Having freed the digestive tract (which has little nutritional value) from the carcass, drag it away so it doesn't lure predators like jackals to your camp. In an emergency such as a sudden sandstorm, the camel's cavity can be used as a temporary shelter. Although this might sound a little drastic, survival is all about going the extra mile and pushing yourself beyond your normal limits. Sheer willpower can often see you through. Camel dung is dry and will usually take a spark so it can be used to start a fire. You can then cook (on a flat stone) the meat for fuel and to raise morale.

If you reach the foothills of the Atlas, beware of flash floods. It can be raining hundreds of miles away and this water will suddenly rush through the dry riverbeds. The oleander bush only grows near water and may look appetising but don't be fooled by the beautiful plants and innocuous leaves: everything about it is highly poisonous, including the sap which can pollute water systems.

If you need to find another source, move up the dry riverbeds. Keep an eye and ear out for any birds as they like to drink at dawn and dusk and never stray too far from water.

If you find water in among the gorges, drink your fill and top up any containers you have. If you're lucky, you should come across old caravan trails used by the nomads and Berbers for trading between outposts. Some will lead to settlements and most will have shelters on the route. If you find a village, you should finally be safe.

The Namib Desert on the Skeleton Coast in southwest Africa presents its own challenges. There's very little in the way of fresh water but you can scavenge on the beach for rope and bits of timber that have come from the countless wrecks. Always be on the lookout for scorpions, however. Large tails and small pincers mean they're usually highly venomous.

There is a way to make water using a solar still. Dig a pit on the beach beyond the high tide mark and pour in as much seawater or urine as you can. Then place your mug or any other receptacle in the centre of the still, cover it with a plastic bag from the wreckage on the beach and weigh it down with rocks. Once you've sealed the edges with sand, place a small rock in the centre of the bag above your mug. The heat will force pure water to condense on the bag and drip into your mug. If you're lucky, you could make two pints (1.25 litres) of water a day, but you'll need more than five times this if you're going to survive for any length of time.

(No matter how great the temptation, you should never drink seawater. It has such a high concentration of salt that you will always crave more. The salt will also draw water from your body's cells and other tissues, particularly the kidneys, severely dehydrating them and causing them to break down. The result is delirium and then death.)

If you're stranded near the coast, you should be able to find mussels and other shellfish to live on, but they must always be cooked to kill harmful bacteria. You'll need a fire and a camp in place before the sun drops because the temperature can fall by as much as 56°C (100°F) overnight. Mussels can be cooked

in the embers and are a good source of protein.

If you have to head inland to be rescued, aim for high ground to look for water courses or signs of civilisation. Animals need water too, so if you come across a series of tracks it might be worth following them to the source. Keep an eye out for puff adders though. They rarely give way for people and will strike when approached. If you don't die from the initial anaphylactic shock, the toxins in its venom rot human flesh and can cause gangrene.

The snake is edible though, but you will need to take extreme care during the kill. It's best done from a distance with a rock, but always pin the head down before you remove it to make sure you can't be bitten. The fangs can still deliver venom after death so bury or burn the head immediately. The flesh is a good source of protein and can be eaten raw, but cooking it for half an hour in a bush oven using the embers from a fire will make it taste much better. Take the remaining meat with you for later.

The dollar bush (so called because

**Centre:** The deadly Sahara.

**Far Right:** Robert Bogucki was found after six weeks in the Australian outback.

its leaves look like coins) is a valuable water source. The leaves are thick and juicy and contain plenty of fluid. Crush them and squeeze the bitter water into your mouth or bottle. Riverbeds that look dry can sometimes contain water in ancient pools. If there's only mud, try digging down a little. The muddy water can be filtered with bushman grass and then sucked up through the hollow tubes. Goa plants contain about a cupful of water so you should look out for them. Water can also collect in the crooks of trees and can be sucked through hollow grass.

The sand bushmen themselves live to the east beyond the Brandberg Mountain. They are hunter-gatherers who know how to survive in the harshest climate on earth. They comb the bush looking for faint animal tracks called spoors. When they find one, they'll follow it to the animal's burrow and ram their sharp barbed spears into the hole to complete the kill. Porcupines might fight back however, so it pays to be careful. If you come across these desert dwellers, you should soon make it back to civilisation.

# The Search for Oneself

In 1999 American fire-fighter Robert Bogucki wandered into the Great Sandy Desert of Western Australia to get closer to nature and find out a bit about himself, and to make his peace with God. His seemingly innocent hike soon turned into a major search-and-rescue operation after he became lost. His bike and camping gear were found on a desert track but the Aboriginal people failed to track him any further. After 12 days the recovery operation was called off as locals knew no one could survive that long. Bogucki's family didn't give up however, and they recruited specialist trackers to continue the hunt.

He was eventually found in the Edgar Ranges by a news helicopter after 43 days. In that time he'd wandered 250 miles (400km) from his starting point. He survived by eating a range of flowers and plants, and from sipping strained muddy water, but he'd still lost 44 pounds (20kg) in bodyweight. He was taken to Broome Hospital but was later released in remarkable physical condition considering the nature of his ordeal. In fact, other than the weight loss, he only had a few scratches on his feet and back. He was not sunburned or suffering the effects of exposure.

It is believed that his family helped pay the AUS$22,000 cost of the recovery effort, as well as contributing towards the US$50,000 charged by the trackers flown in from the United States.

# Surviving at Sea

If your boat sinks or you've fallen overboard from your cruise ship, you may start to panic if you think rescue might not happen immediately. Indeed, survival at sea is one of the toughest challenges a person is likely to face, and without adequate resources it is extremely difficult. But improvisation and positive thinking have helped many a castaway live to tell their tale. If you have a means of signalling when you hit the water – flare, smoke grenade, sea dye or torch – use it immediately to attract attention.

If you have nothing with you, your best bet is to hope that someone has seen you go in and that they will raise the alarm. Try to make yourself as visible as possible because you will be difficult to spot from the bridge or deck of a large passenger ship. If your boat has sunk and you are alone, you should try to head for land (another reason why it's vital to know exactly where you are at all times) because the coast, even if it is only a small deserted island, can provide you with everything you need to survive for a long period. Large human populations live by the sea and they use the water for pleasure and trade, so this is another good reason to find land.

Clouds rarely form over the open ocean so, if you can see any, head for them as they're likely to be over

**Above:** Smoke Signal.

land (where moist air has been pushed up until it condenses). Storms and lightning are also more likely over land. Birds rarely cross large expanses of open water, so follow them later in the day when they're heading back to the nest after feeding. As you approach land, try to spot the best place to come ashore; large breakers, cliffs and shallow reefs should be avoided. Don't fight the sea. If the currents are sweeping you along the coast in a rip, go with them and swim or paddle parallel to the shore gradually angling your way in until you reach the beach.

**Above:** A recreation of Poon Lim's raft.

If you don't make land quickly, your chances of survival are extremely slim and you risk hypothermia, severe sunburn and heatstroke, blindness (water reflects sunlight in the same way that snow does) and dehydration. If you're in a raft, you will need to provide protection from the sun in warmer climes and the cold and wind in others, so, as usual, you should start your quest for survival with shelter. (If you don't have a raft, keep your clothes on unless you're struggling for buoyancy. Trousers can be used as a buoyancy aid if you tie the ankle openings closed and then fill the legs with air. Swim slowly and steadily to avoid exhaustion, overheating or hypothermia – depending on conditions.)

Manufacture some sort of overhead protection as soon as possible, then cover up with clothes, sunglasses and a hat, dry your clothes as best you can, and make sure that all personal waste goes over the side. Hygiene is a vital ingredient for survival at sea. Bad weather is another challenge you'll face. If the raft has a sea anchor, use it. If not, one can be jury-rigged with a bag of clothes and a few lines.

The idea is to create drag so that your vessel remains stable.

You should be prepared to collect fresh water from day one and always ration whatever supplies you have unless it is plentiful. Use anything you can to collect rain: shoes, plastic bags and clothes can all store water, but try to devise a guttering system so that your main supply can be stored in one secure place. If you're stranded in colder latitudes, old icebergs (which will be bluer and more rounded) should be salt-free. Fish eyes are a good source of water. But you should never drink seawater. Its high salt and mineral content will have you craving more, but it will draw water from your body's cells until they can no longer function. This leads to kidney failure, delirium and then death.

In extreme situations, however, a little seawater can be mixed with freshwater to help replace the salts you lose when sweating, and up to a pint a day (but no more) of seawater, or water contaminated by engine oil, can also be absorbed via an enema as not all of the salt content or impurities will enter the body. As you're bypassing the stomach, you

**Above:** Mussels, sea snails and limpets clinging to a rock.

won't vomit either. Some rafts have solar stills as part of their survival equipment, and some also have reverse osmosis kits that can provide clean, salt-free water from seawater. Turtle blood can be drunk, as can the spinal fluid of most fish.

If you've managed to source water, food will be your next problem. Clearly, your diet at sea is going to be largely made up of fish. Hooks can be fashioned from pins, wire, wood and bone. Try to make the line as thin as possible and attach a shiny lure near the hook. An improvised spear can be used to harpoon curious fish that come to inspect your raft. Use their guts as bait and to 'chum' the area around your raft as this will attract more fish. Some tropical fish

they've been lured close enough by your fish bait. Small quantities of seaweed can be eaten (not too much as its salt content is high), and the tiny crustaceans that live amongst it should be okay raw. Other shellfish will need to be cooked however as they contain harmful bacteria.

If, when you make land, you discover that the coastline or island is uninhabited, you will have to continue fending for yourself. You should forage for limpets, whelks, barnacles, sea snails, crabs, oysters, clams and mussels at low tide in rock pools. It is usually best to leave them for a couple of days so that they purge themselves of any toxins. A pair of tights makes a good net to trawl for smaller fry. Octopus and squid can also be eaten, although you should cook them first and avoid the beak and guts.

(particularly the puffer fish family) may be toxic, but deepwater fish should all be okay. Take care when handling those with sharp fins, scales, spikes and stingers.

Seabirds, too, are a good source of food. They are also usually a sign that you could be close to land as most birds won't stray too far from the nest. Try to snare them once

As with all survival situations, making fire is crucial for morale, providing clean drinking water, cooking and signalling. The latter will become the most important if people are out looking for you but don't assume that you have been seen from a ship or aircraft until you're actually being rescued.

# Adrift

In 1982, Steven Callahan set sail from the Canary Islands and headed across the Atlantic to the Caribbean. A week later his boat, *Napoleon Solo*, sank in a storm after hitting a whale and he was forced to make his escape in a six-foot inflatable raft with only a T-shirt, three pounds of food, eight pints (five litres) of water and precious little gear from the boat.

He soon exhausted these meagre rations and was forced to make water from solar stills and by collecting rain, which gave him around a pint (half a litre) per day. He learned to live like an aquatic caveman, his water collecting routine only interrupted by spear fishing, snaring the odd bird, navigating and making repairs to the raft. He then drifted for 76 days and 1,800 miles (2,700km) before he reached the Bahamas.

He was eventually rescued by fishermen who noticed that the raft had become a little ecosystem. His story of survival is remarkable in that he had to provide food and water, as well as sheltering from the elements and keeping the raft afloat, for more than two months. It would have been easy for his morale to collapse and for him to give up but he stayed mentally strong and ultimately prevailed despite losing a third of his bodyweight.

# Torpedoed

While he was working as a steward on the *SS Ben Lomond* during World War II, Poon Lim's ship was torpedoed by the *U-172*. Lim escaped into the water before the ship's boilers exploded and she sank. After a couple of hours he found a small life-raft that had some biscuits and a 70-pint (40-litre) jug of water.

He rationed the food and water but soon ran out. He used a small tarpaulin to collect rainwater to drink and fashioned a hook from the wiring in a small torch to try to catch fish. He then used a little hemp rope to make a line.

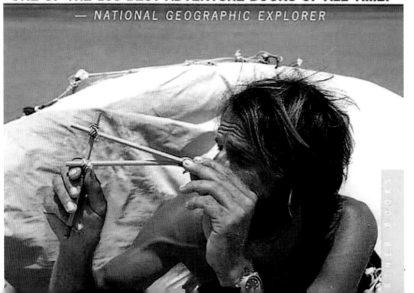

The classic *New York Times* bestseller

# ADRIFT

## STEVEN CALLAHAN

Seventy-six Days Lost at Sea

with a new epilogue

"ONE OF THE 100 BEST ADVENTURE BOOKS OF ALL TIME."
— NATIONAL GEOGRAPHIC EXPLORER

1885

He caught several fish but once was only saved from certain death by catching a bird and drinking its blood. He also managed to club the odd shark (their livers and other organs contain valuable minerals).

Although he spotted several ships, aircraft and another U-boat, Lim wasn't rescued until he was picked up by Brazilian fishermen 133 days later. Although he'd only lost 20 pounds (9kg) in weight, he spent a month in hospital recovering. His record still stands as the longest any single person has survived at sea on a raft.

In late 2005 three Mexican shark fishermen ran out of fuel and their boat was taken west into the Pacific by the currents. Nine months later they were finally rescued off the Marshall Islands. They had survived on rainwater, urine, sea turtles and raw fish.

# Castaway

When Alexander Selkirk complained to his captain that their ship, the *Cinque Ports*, was un-seaworthy in 1704, William Dampier told him he was free to leave. Having been dropped off on the uninhabited island of Juan Fernández off the coast of Chile in the South Pacific, Selkirk immediately regretted offending his captain. But Dampier wouldn't allow him back onboard and condemned Selkirk to four years on a desert island.

Selkirk was extremely resourceful however. He ate shellfish, feral goats that had been introduced by earlier expeditions to the archipelago, wild turnips, cabbage and berries. He domesticated cats to keep him safe from rats and became a dab hand with his knife, with which he fashioned new clothes from goatskin.

Four years later he was rescued by the *Duke*, a ship piloted by non other than Dampier. Selkirk's story was headline news and Daniel Defoe based *Robinson Crusoe* on the story of the real-life castaway. Juan Fernández has since been renamed Robinson Crusoe Island.

# ALSO AVAILABLE IN THE LITTLE BOOK SERIES

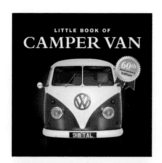
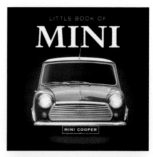
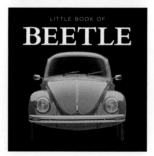

## ALSO AVAILABLE IN THE LITTLE BOOK SERIES

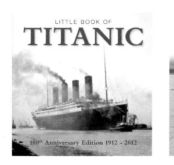

**The pictures in this book were provided courtesy of the following**:

WIKIMEDIA COMMONS

Design & Artwork: SCOTT GIARNESE

Published by: DEMAND MEDIA LIMITED & G2 ENTERTAINMENT LIMITED

Publishers: JASON FENWICK & JULES GAMMOND

Written by: LIAM MCCANN